BURNING MOM

ALSO BY MIEKO OUCHI

Mieko Ouchi: Two Plays
I Am For You

BURNING MOM
MIEKO OUCHI

PLAYWRIGHTS CANADA PRESS
TORONTO

Burning Mom © Copyright 2023 by Mieko Ouchi

For professional or amateur production rights, please contact:
Ian Arnold at Catalyst TCM
PO Box 98074, RPO Queen and Carlaw, Toronto, ON M4M 3L9
416.568.8673 | ian@catalysttcm.com

LIBRARY AND ARCHIVES CANADA CATALOGUING IN PUBLICATION
Title: Burning mom / Mieko Ouchi.
Names: Ouchi, Mieko, author.
Description: First edition.
Identifiers: Canadiana (print) 20230183875 | Canadiana (ebook) 20230184006 | ISBN 9780369104342 (softcover) | ISBN 9780369104359 (PDF) | ISBN 9780369104366 (EPUB)
Classification: LCC PS8579.U26 B87 2023 | DDC C812/.6—dc23

Playwrights Canada Press operates on land which is the ancestral home of the Anishinaabe Nations (Ojibwe / Chippewa, Odawa, Potawatomi, Algonquin, Saulteaux, Nipissing, and Mississauga), the Wendat, and the members of the Haudenosaunee Confederacy (Mohawk, Oneida, Onondaga, Cayuga, Seneca, and Tuscarora), as well as Metis and Inuit peoples. It always was and always will be Indigenous land.

We acknowledge the financial support of the Canada Council for the Arts, the Ontario Arts Council (OAC), Ontario Creates, and the Government of Canada for our publishing activities.

For Eugene

Burning Mom was workshopped for fu-GEN Theatre Company as part of the 2016 Walk the Walk Festival and with the Royal Manitoba Theatre Centre for Prairie Theatre Exchange's 2019 Festival of New Works. It was also supported by Workshop West Playwrights' Theatre and the Canada Council for the Arts while Mieko was the 2018–2019 Playwright-in-Residence.

The play was first produced by the Royal Manitoba Theatre Centre at the John Hirsch Mainstage, Winnipeg, from April 26 to May 20, 2023, with the following cast and creative team:

Dorothy Ouchi: Lisa Horner
Dorothy Alternate: Megan McArton

Director: Mieko Ouchi
Set Designer: Brian Perchaluk
Costume Designer: Linda Beech
Lighting Designer: Larry Isacoff
Sound Designer: Ashley Au
Video Designer: Cameron Davis
Assistant Director: Zanifa Rasool
Assistant Set Designer: Joyce Licup
Stage Manager: Margaret Brook
Assistant Stage Manager: Michael Duggan
Apprentice Stage Manager: Jazz Marcelino

CAST

Dorothy: A woman in her sixties

TIME

2010 / 2011

ACT I

A woman stands on stage. She wipes her eyes with a crumpled Kleenex balled up in her hand. She puts it in her pocket.

Bucars is one of Alberta's largest RV dealerships. It's in the north-west corner of Calgary, on the way to Airdrie. They sell RVs, service RVs, and store RVs.

And that's where it was.

The Jaguar. Twenty-six feet long. Open plan. Queen-size bed. With side tables. An oven and microwave. Dining room with a table and an upholstered bench seat that turns into a second bed. A bathroom with a toilet, sink, *and* a shower. Heater and air conditioning.

It was for our retirement. Eugene was going to be stepping down from his duties at the Art College at the end of the next semester and we had so many plans. For years we'd go out in our little old camper with boxes of watercolours and paint and draw for a week or two. Before that we'd done it out of a pup tent and Eugene's old Beamer. We'd gone all over Alberta and BC and even made a trip up to Haida Gwaii, north of Vancouver, for two weeks in old-growth forest.

But that was the old us. The new us had a shiny RV with the stickers still on it.

We got it home from Bucars and I poured myself a glass of wine and Eugene got a beer and we went to sit in it. Right there, in front of the house, and then Eugene said:

This kind of feels like an old folks' home.

It was the decor. Somehow it had looked okay when it was surrounded by other RVs. It's like when you buy clothes in Florida. They look okay there because they fit in. It's hot and sunny and everyone else is wearing them, and somehow it makes a kind of sense. But then you get home and wonder how the hell you ended up with gold lamé sandals covered in sequin starfish.

That was the RV.

Now we were home, the full effect hit us like a two-by-four. Everything was done in pastel shades of peach, grey, and pink. There were hideous puffy upholstered valances above every window. The bedspread and bench seat matched. The carpets and wallpaper matched. It was like going to brunch in 1983.

The colours, I think, were meant to soothe us. To calm us. To put us in the happy, relaxed place that people of our age are supposed to be in their retirement.

No, I said to Eugene. This is worse than an old folks' home. It looks like a funeral home.

Well, he said, *we can change that.* And he reached over and ripped a valance off the window.

We ripped the rest of them off and I made some simple paper shades out of Japanese washi paper instead. Eugene picked some small pieces of art from our studios and hung those, and I started on a new quilt that would replace the original bed-spread. I called it my Prairie quilt. Log-cabin pattern in blues for the sky, golds for the fields, and greys and greens for the mountains and trees.

And it started to look like us.

I loved that RV.

 Beat.

But the thing about RVs is . . . No. The thing they *don't tell you* about RVs is . . . they are conceived, built, and sold with the inten-tion that they are driven, handled, and parked by at least two grown-up humans.

 Beat.

So of course . . . as we began to . . . sort through things, the topic of the RV came up. The kids were wondering what to do with it.

Do with it? I said. Well I'm not getting rid of it. We just got it.

My son Kevin said:

But there's absolutely no way you can drive that thing. I don't think I can even drive that thing.

My daughter Mieko said:

Why don't you sell it and get a camping van, it would be so much easier and safer.

My son Jason said:

Don't look at me. You all know I hate camping.

But I didn't want to get rid of it. I don't know what possessed me, but I said no. No! I love the RV. We had big plans to use it, and I'm going to do just that.

They all threw up their hands.

But Jason and Kevin's friend Dan had a suggestion. Dan was over watching a rerun of *Tremors* and he was kind of a car guy, and he had overheard our entire RV exchange from his seat in the family room where he often sat after driving over from his house two blocks away.

He tossed this out: *Well, Dorth, if you want to learn how to drive it, just find an empty parking lot and practise. That's what guys do. They get a big vehicle? They just find an empty parking lot and practise.*

Guys *do* that? He looked at me like I was crazy.

Course they do. I mean, what can happen in an empty parking lot, right?

Beat.

She looks out at us. Finally she relents.

Okay . . . I'm going totell you what can happen in an empty parking lot.

For a while I worked at Fabricland. You know, part-time for some extra money after I retired from daycare? Well, I usually drove our little Honda to work, but one Monday, for some reason Eugene needed it and he told me to take the truck.

I've never liked driving the truck. It's so high, and I'm so short— not great when you're wearing a skirt or pants without elastic. And it has a stick shift on the column of the wheel, you know, like old cars used to, and that always freaks me out.

Anyway, the other thing you have to keep in mind, the thing you need to know, is that we had just been camping. At that time, we had our first camper. One of those old-fashioned basic ones, you know, the ones that sit right on the bed of the truck? We had just gotten back the night before, on Sunday, and we hadn't had time to drive it back out to the RV storage.

Now Fabricland is at the north end of Northland Mall. Since the mall has been getting busier, the year before they built a two-storey parkade at that end. The door on the second floor leads right to Fabricland. It's very convenient.

So . . . I didn't think twice as I pulled into the lot and headed for my usual spot.

The explosion was heard for at least four square blocks. From Winston Churchill High School right over to the car dealership on the other side of the mall. I don't actually know that for sure, but I think that's pretty accurate, because one of the guys rubbernecking had his dealership jacket on.

A camper that is ripped off the back of a truck is kind of like a shell that's been torn off a snail. No, more like the top half of an oyster shell that's been ripped off an oyster, because you see everything that's inside. Because everything that was inside is now . . . outside.

By the time the police arrived, I was crying so hard I couldn't even see. But through my sobs, I heard a voice saying:

Mrs. Ouchi?

All I could think was, that police officer knows my name. Oh God, I'm going to jail.

Mrs. Ouchi?

I'm going to jail for destroying a camper and a truck and a parkade, because while I was waiting I had begun to notice that there were several large pieces of the parkade next to me, right where they had fallen off the beam above the ramp.

Mrs. Ouchi? It's Leonard.

Leonard?

I went to school with Jason and Kevin. Eugene coached me in hockey. Peewee.

The nice-looking young officer did start to look familiar. Leonard?

Yeah. It looks like you had a little interaction with the parkade?

I was now hiccupping as I tried to stop sobbing. A-hu, A-hu, are you going to charge me?

No . . . clearly this was an accident. No one was hurt. And this is what insurance is for, right? Now, let me go write this up and you call Eugene.

No. God. No. I don't want Eugene and the kids to know what I've done. But I don't say that. I just nod and watch him walk back to his car, to his partner who has taken off his hat and is staring at the decapitated camper in disbelief.

Hey.

It's a middle-aged man in khaki shorts and a T-shirt with a bag from Best Buy in one hand and an Iced Capp in the other. He's stopped, like everyone else, gawking at the crime scene. He looks like someone who would roll his eyes at the guy next to him and mouth "lady drivers." But that's *not* what he does. Instead, he does a little gesture. A little . . .

She gestures.

... for me to come closer. He looks around.

Don't beat yourself up too hard. I did that once too you know.

And he chin nods towards the camper.

The important thing is . . . don't give up.

And then he nods again. And he walks away.

    She watches him go.

So . . . you can see why I wasn't keen to return to the parking lot at Northland Mall. Nope. Northland's definitely off the list.

But Dan's words stuck with me, so I start looking around Calgary, analyzing it in a way I have never done before.

Brentwood Co-op. No. Clear line of sight from the LRT. Too humiliating.

Crowfoot Crossing. God no! It's all built on a series of intersecting curlicues. Plus, they have a lot of bars, so they're always busy, even at night. Not good.

But then I suddenly remember. Across from Bucars, where the RV is stored, in the middle of some fields, twenty minutes north of Calgary, is CrossIron Mills. A mega complex of factory-outlet box stores anchored by an enormous Bass Pro Shops, a massive multiplex cinema and . . .

. . . the biggest damn parking lot in southern Alberta.

And that is how I became the only student enrolled in the Dorothy Ouchi School for Advanced RV Driving.

I commit myself to one week of practise. Surely by the end of the week, I will know if I am able to drive the RV myself, if I should keep the rig or give it up like my kids want me to.

One week. I have one week.

Monday.

After an early supper, I drive my pickup to Bucars, and a nice young fellow takes my keys, drives it into the storage area, and pulls it out with the trailer already attached. It takes way less time than I anticipated. And it's way longer than I remember.

She's all yours, he says.

She *is* all mine. All twenty-six damn feet of her.

I get in and try not to let the kid see that I've started crying. My hands are shaking, but I can hear Eugene scoffing at the challenge like he always did. *C'mon, Dorth. How hard can this be?*

The kid is waiting, so I put it in gear with a jolt, and slowly, very slowly, pull out and inch across Highway 2 into the north parking lot of CrossIron Mills.

I try to think through the worst-case scenario. If I'm doing something wrong, they'll come and kick me out and I'll just have to drive back to Bucars. But what if Bucars is closed? That's okay. I'll sleep in the RV outside the gate until they open in the morning. Yeah. I'll tell them I've been called for jury duty at the last minute, and I just have to put it back in storage.

Sounds like a plan.

It takes thirty minutes to back into my first parking spot. It makes no sense. Finally, I realize to turn left you have to turn the wheel to the right. Why? Argh. I'm concentrating so hard on staying within the yellow lines . . .

A knock at the window.

Can I help you?

A man in uniform is at my window. I try to catch my breath, but instead all my inner thoughts just pour right out. My husband and I bought this RV and we had all these plans, but now . . . my family want me to sell it, but I just can't bear the thought of that, so I'm here to practise driving it. I've committed to one solid week of practise to see if I can do it. If I can, I'll keep it, but if I can't, I'll listen to my kids and sell the darn thing off once and for all.

The man didn't say a word. I think he needed a minute to fully take in what I had said. Finally, he takes a few steps back and checks out the Jaguar. Like, really takes her all in. Then he makes a gesture like a reverse circle in the air.

You need to practise backing up.

Turns out he actually knows quite a bit about trailers and how to drive them. He used to drive a school bus when he first came to Canada. He's very helpful. By the end of the night, I find out his name is Parveen. I'm Dorothy, I say. It's so good to meet you. I try to thank him, but that just seems to embarrass him. He backs away and gives me a little nod with his eyes closed like, "No problem. No problem."

That week I practise every night for about two and a half hours each time. And each night Parveen comes out pretty much as soon as I get there. I must come up on a screen in the security office. I can only imagine what he says to the other guards.

Oh dear. The crazy lady is back, parking and reparking in strange configurations. I'll go talk to her.

And there he'd be. Making that gesture again.

By Thursday he brought a friend. Dave. Dave says, *I heard what you were doing. Just wanted to say hi.*

I'm so grateful, I think I prattle on a bit. Oh my God, I really have to thank you guys for letting me do this. And not making fun of me. You're both so kind. I am going to write a letter to the mall and tell them how kind you are. And how much you've helped me. Oh but don't worry. I won't tell them how much time you've spent out here. Your supervisor probably shouldn't know how many hours you've been out here? Parveen's eyes get wide. Dave says.

I am his supervisor.

The next night, Dave comes again. And again. By Friday, he brings three other guards. They all seem to know my story. They cheer when I back into a stall successfully my first time out without anyone's help. It takes a while, but I am definitely between all of the yellow lines. Parveen . . . has a grin on his face. He looks almost . . . proud. And then he hands me something.

This is from all of us. A gift card to Starbucks. *You improved more than we ever thought you would.*

It's true, says Dave. *You're the most dedicated parker we've ever seen. Good luck to ya.*

And that's it. My week is up. My confidence is up. Time to take this little show on the road.

To give myself a final boost I head to the Chapters at Dalhousie Station. I walk right in and tell a girl there that I need a book that will really inspire me. And she tells me to buy this new book *Wild.* So I do, and then as an afterthought, I go and get myself a small latte at the Starbucks attached. Using my gift card.

You know what? Add a shot of vanilla. Why the hell not.

And then I do it. I go camping.

I decide to start in High River. A tiny town southeast of Calgary. I figure with the pull of the mountains on the west, no one will be there. Perfect.

My hands are aching by the time I arrive at the visitor's centre. I cheer because I'm able to just pull right up to the curb outside. No backing up. No parking required. No problem.

I need a campground, I tell the young man at the desk. I lean on the counter, trying to sound casual. You know . . . something with no trees. Nice big lots. Not too many hills.

The young kid, he couldn't have been more than seventeen, he says he doesn't know anything about that, but . . . *I think there's a nice one down by the river? The Lions Club runs it?*

I nod coolly. Any cul-de-sacs?

He seems thrown by my question. Again, he's not sure.

Okay, I say. Where is it?

You been here before?

Now that's an interesting question. I'm not sure what to tell him, so I just say: Yeah . . . A long time ago.

He shrugs. Draws me a little map and I'm back on the road.

At first I'm not sure. But then I start recognizing things. The houses have hardly changed, like that one, my best friend Betty lived there. And oh my God, that one . . . that's Robby Boyd's house. Once I see the lot though, I know for sure. My old house. I haven't been back since . . . I don't even know. 1954 maybe? We left when I was so little. I haven't thought about it in years.

And there at the end of the street is the faded sign. Lions Club Campground. One block away from my old house. It's got to be a sign.

I pull in. And that's when I realize that kid knew diddly-squat about campgrounds.

There are trees everywhere. There are no pull through spaces. Okay, there are no hills, but shit. It's getting dark and I'm hooped. I'll have to back up to even get out. Shit. Shit. Shit.

* * * * *

An older couple sit watching me like they're watching their favourite TV show.

They watch as I climb out of the truck and hold my hands out, like I've seen my daughter do, like a filmmaker, measuring the space between trees like I'm lining up a shot. Like I know exactly what I'm doing.

Yep, I say, nodding vigorously to myself, and to the old couple, as if all this makes perfect sense. I clamber back into the truck. Well shit, Dorth. You're just going to have to do it. And with an audience my very first time.

There's a knock on the window.

Oh God. It's the husband.

You want some help?

When I arrived I was so distracted by sheer panic, I didn't really look at their RV, but I can now make out that it is a huge all-in-one, the size of a shipping container.

These spots are tight. Don't try and back this thing in by yourself.

I'm about to get out, to explain that I've changed my mind, that I'm actually going to go back home, but he stops the door and shuts it again firmly.

Sorry, that came out wrong, dear. What I meant was, you're gonna need a spotter, rig this big. You can do it. I'll just guide you in.

And so thirty . . . to . . . forty-five minutes later . . . I'm in.

I may have gotten a little ahead of myself. Practising in a parking lot really meant I was only ready to park in . . . other parking lots. I hadn't really taken into consideration things like . . . trees.

The old guy breaks my thought bubble by coughing into a hanky. He gives me a big thumbs-up and heads back to his chair where he drinks a full bottle of water. He and his wife watch me put the blocks clumsily under the hitch. Then put out my small Astroturf carpet, my camping side table with a lantern, and my book. And finally, my one single camping chair.

   Beat.

Later that night over glasses of wine he confides in me.

Parking these damn things can be tricky sometimes.

His very sweet wife passes me a plate of ham-and-cheese roll-ups.

Oh yes. Very tricky. I have to spot him all the time too, you know.

He tells me that their son just bought an RV as well.

I tried to teach him how to back in, but that boy never listens. At least . . . you listen.

I can picture their son, a strapping young guy, just like my own two boys, brushing off his dad's instructions with a long-suffering nod. *Yeah, yeah, Dad.* His wife fishes something out of her purse. A small photo.

Here he is. He's sixty-three.

She smiles as she brushes some Kleenex dust off his balding head. But that's practically my age. In my head I do the math. If he's sixty-three, that would put both of them . . . in their early to mid eighties. Jesus.

You like to camp alone, dear?

She's caught me off guard. This is the question I've been fearing most. I've practised what to say . . .

I've um . . . I've always wanted a camper . . . so I taught myself how to drive the RV and I've been practising in a parking lot for a week and this is my first time camping by myself.

She pats my hand. *Well, good for you, dear. That's brave, you know.*

That night, after I've gone back to the RV and I'm alone with all my unopened painting supplies, I try reading that damn book *Wild*, but after a while I give up and I think about Eugene and I cry until I can't cry anymore and then I dry my eyes and I think.

That sweet old lady is right. It is brave. And camping *is* good for me. And looking at the paints strewn across the table, an image suddenly pops into my head. An image of . . . Emily Carr. I must have seen that photo back when I was in art school. Emily alone, in the deep forest, covered in paint, working.

And I think, well shit, Dorth. Okay, I'm no Emily Carr, but if she was able to haul all her supplies, and a tent, and food, all that stuff that she needed to do her work, out into the middle of the forest by herself, so can I. I can't give up. Not until I destroy this damn thing or myself.

    Beat.

And that's when I get the idea.

* * * * *

As soon as I get back to Calgary, I call the kids over.

I have something important to tell you.

They all immediately look concerned.

Everything is okay. I've just been thinking. We've all been so stressed out with everything going on . . . I think we should go on a family trip together. You know, so we can regroup a little, and have some time to gather our thoughts. We've been through so much. I think it's . . . important.

My daughter's eyes light up. *You mean like . . . go to Mexico or something?* I can feel relief coming off her in waves. Dreams of an all-inclusive are already dancing in her head.

. . . Um . . . well not exactly.

My sons are also having visions.

Kevin says, *Maybe we could go to Vancouver? Ooh . . . the island. Sushi?*

Jason says, *How about Hawaii? You know, for some golf?*

Uhm. Again, not quite what I have in mind.

Kids. I think we should go to Burning Man.

> *Beat.*

$$\star \ \star \ \star \ \star \ \star$$

What?

In my RV.

Don't worry, I say. I can drive it now. I've been . . . practising.

We sit in the family room for a long while in a kind of confused and uneasy hush.

Mieko says nothing, her brows furrowed. She's the oldest and a worrier. I can see she's wondering if I've truly gone and lost it this time. Off the edge. Taken over by grief.

My middle son, Jason, is rubbing his head like he has a bad headache. Like he's trying to take what I just said and rub it into some kind of sense. In his world, moms aren't supposed to say things like "let's go to Burning Man."

My youngest son Kevin is different. He has a strange look on his face. He's staring off into space. From time to time, he shakes his head. Like he can't believe what he just heard. Finally, he says one word: *Hunh.*

That seems to break the ice.

When is this happening? That's Mieko. Always practical.

Fall, I say. Early September.

But that's only a few months away. I'm directing a play. It's way too late for me to replace myself.

I look at Jason.

I don't know, Mom. I've missed so many days, I can't tell the bank now I'm up and leaving for what . . . ?

Just ten days, I say. Plus travel.

To hang out in a party in the desert?

I turn to Kevin. He's my only hope. He's the only person I know who has actually been to Burning Man.

Hunh, he says again. You . . . *want to go to Burning Man.*

Yes. I do. I do. I want to go.

But, Mama, you know it's not like regular camping, right?

Of *course*, I say. Everyone knows that.

It's ten days in a desert with no showers.

Absolutely.

Like there's no . . . regular type RV *hookups and stuff.*

That doesn't bother me.

And you know it's an art festival. So there's nudity, and alternative lifestyles, and people do things like take drugs and stuff . . .

Kevin. I wasn't born yesterday.

He shakes his head. He's trying to wrap his head around it all.

Ma, why do you want to go?

How do I even . . .

    She takes a deep breath.

Kevin, after you went that last time, Eugene was so curious. Do you remember when you came over for dinner and told us all about it, and he asked you so many questions? Well that night, when we went to bed, he said, *You know what, Dorth . . . one day, we should go to Burning Man.*

She laughs.

It just seemed so far-fetched, but I don't know . . . somehow that stuck with me. Somewhere in the back of my brain, that thought has been sitting there, just waiting all this time. Until now. Well, actually, until the other night. In a campground. When it just popped back into my head.

The kids are staring at me, trying to understand. So I . . . I keep going.

Kids. I want to face my fears. Prove something to myself. That I'm not too old. That I'm not past adventures. I just . . . I don't know why . . . but I need to know I can do it.

And . . . I have the RV.

Finally, Kevin speaks.

You really, seriously, *want to go?*

She nods.

Yes. I do.

Well . . . okay then . . . I'll take you.

* * * * *

Word got out fast. I think Kevin must have put something in Facebook, because pretty soon, my brother and sister-in-law were calling, and some of my nieces seemed to know. A lady at the Y even mentioned it. Then Kevin told me we'd been invited to share a camp with some of his friends who build speakers for big music festivals . . . you know, like . . . *raves*.

It'll be cool, Mom. They're taking a huge rig down there on a semi and setting up a sound stage.

To share the cost, he'd also found a friend to come along, named Hilary. He tries to explain to me how they know each other. It's very complicated, but I'm pretty sure she's the ex-girlfriend of one of his really good friends.

Are you an item? The kid is perennially single.

God, Mom, don't be so weird. She's just a girl who is not my girl-friend, but who is a friend. Guys are allowed to do that now, you know.

And that's how our little group came to be. Me, my son, and a girl who is not his girlfriend.

Preparing for Burning Man.

First thing's first. Kevin finds two used bikes for us. Only problem is, to get one the right size for my legs, mine is clearly meant for a ten-to-twelve-year-old and has the word "Dazzle" emblazoned on the centre bar. I haven't been on a bike in years.

Kevin announces that we need to decorate them.

What? Why?

So no one takes them.

Is someone going to steal my bike?

Nooo, they won't steal them, Mom, but at the festival it's just kind of okay for people to take spare bikes and use them to get around. They just "borrow" them. But if you decorate your bike, it's clear it's an "art bike" and people won't take it. They'll take a plain one instead . . .

Well, I don't want anyone to take Dazzle, even if they are just borrowing her. I'm already attached. So I head to the dollar store. A huge felt daisy with wire inside seems a good place to start. I also pick up . . . different coloured electrical tape and, in a moment of inspiration, some fluorescent streamers for my handlebars.

In the end, Dazzle is adorable. Kevin's bike on other hand is . . . disgusting. It's covered in brown fake fur from top to bottom and looks like the bicycle version of a Wookie. He calls it "Elmo."

Check, he says. *Bikes are done.*

I head to Mountain Equipment Co-op with the shopping list Kevin has made for me.

Headlamp. Check.

Goggles. Check.

CamelBak. For water. Check.

Then, Superstore for the next three necessities. Spray bottle to cool off. Golf umbrella for shade. Zip-locks to protect the camera from dust. Check. Check. Check.

Then Costco. For sunblock. SPF 65. A three pack. Check. Check. Check.

Kevin comes over and goes through my growing pile:

Good work, Mom. We're getting close. There are a few things we need, but they're things we can't really buy. Like we need something really big for the roof of the RV so we can find it.

I don't know, Kev. The Jag is pretty unique.

Mom. There's gonna be 55,000 people there! There are sandstorms. We're going to be out at night. In the dark. I'm telling you right now, we need something really distinctive.

Fine. After a bit of thinking, I design and build a fish kite. A traditional one for Boys' Day. To honour Eugene's Japanese heritage.

Okay, actually, I end up making two. The first one is about two feet long. But as soon as I finish it, I can hear Eugene. *Shit, Dorothy, the desert is huge. Why're you making your fish so small?*

And he's right. Okay, okay, Eug. Back to the drawing board.

The scale on the second one *is* better. Eight feet long. Three feet high. And mounted on a giant pole. At the last minute, I pull a solar spotlight from my garden and stick it at the bottom to give it some . . . drama.

I imagine Eugene standing next to me, nodding in agreement. No one's gonna miss us in the Nevada desert.

I'm online reading up about the festival and discover that one of the principles of Burning Man is that everyone shares what they have. No commerce is allowed. Only sharing.

Kevin mentioned the last time he went his group had something called Tutu Tuesdays. I mean, I used to work at Fabricland. I make six.

I also make "artist trading cards." Have you ever seen these? It's kind of a neat idea. There is a standard size and artists all over the world make them and give them away. I'd seen some at the Art College and I thought they were so beautiful, so I make a hundred. Hand painted. Each one unique with the symbol of Burning Man on it.

Done. The last two things I needed to do.

Two a.m. The night before we leave. I'm lying in bed but I'm wide awake. That's when I remember Mieko gave me a journal for the trip. It says "Inspire" on the cover.

What the hell do people write in these things anyhow? The only journalling I've ever done was last year, and I don't want to think about that. I was so overwhelmed I couldn't sleep at night, so I would just scribble and scribble and scribble on empty notepads to get the feelings out so I could fall asleep. They're still hidden in the back of the closet. Those were dark, scary, horrible thoughts.

But this journal . . . is different. This one is meant for remembering. Not forgetting. So . . . finally, I write:

How to survive . . .

Then I scratch out "survive" . . . and write a different word . . .

thrive . . .

. . . at Burning Man.

1. Sip water constantly.

Start with the practical. Makes sense in a desert.

2. Think like a four-year-old.

Okay. That is less obvious. But it seems important to enjoy Burning Man . . . right?

3. Watch people.

It occurs to me that half the joy of the festival must be people-watching. Good to remember.

4. Talk to strangers.

It strikes me that some of the things I'm writing down are the things I told my kids *not* to do when they were little. But I guess back then I was trying to save them from danger. Now I'm *looking* for danger. For the outer edge. Okay. Let yourself go, Dorth.

5. Smile and acknowledge others whenever you run into someone, even if they look scary.
6. Breathe.
7. Look at the big sky like a blank canvas.
8. Let go of your judgments about people.
9. Expect goodness.

I'm on a roll. These are *good*.

10. Get better at bike-riding.

Okay, I write that down because I had tried riding Dazzle around our cul-de-sac and it hadn't gone well. Continuing in that vein. But focusing on the positive . . .

11. If you fall off, get up and keep going.
12. Laugh at yourself.

I'm on fire.

13. Dance like a beginner.
14. Walk without a destination.
15. See what happens.

16. Drop all labels you ever put on yourself.
17. Trust your emotions.

Beat.

18. Soak up the exquisiteness of the stars at night.
19. Look for beauty and kindness.
20. Remember that life happens in small special moments. That makes them precious. Notice them. Cherish them. You'll never get those moments back.

A long beat. She is suddenly emotional.

Didn't see that coming.

Well. That's it, I guess. Nothing left to say. Nothing left to prepare.

* * * * *

The road to Burning Man starts early.

As we arranged, Kevin and Hilary come to the house first thing in the morning so we can hit the road by nine. But by the time we unload all their stuff from their cars, and I make everyone a good breakfast, and we pack everything into the RV and the truck, it's lunchtime. But unexpected things happen.

Like Dan. When I come out with my final bag, there he is, standing next to the RV with Jason, Kev, and Hilary.

Dan, what are you doing here? Come to see us off?

Kev was having trouble with the hitch and sent me a text. But I got a question for you. The tires on your truck. When's the last time you changed them?

That was always Eugene's domain. I have no idea, Dan.

Well, Dorth, I don't want to tell you this, but they're completely bald.

After a huge debate, we decide to get new, cheaper tires once we get over the border and into the US.

And that's how, by 9 p.m., in the pitch dark, with bald tires, we're finally ready to hit the road to Burning Man.

But before I can climb in, Kevin announces we have to make an important group decision.

Group Decision Number One: We will all take equal turns driving.

Okay, I know I put up my hand and said yes when he called the vote, but I'm not sure I can do my share. My whole life as an adult, Eugene always drove while I slept. I can't help it. I'm like a toddler in a car seat. As soon as I get in a car, I immediately turn into a drooling, snoring mess. But Kevin was so firm. And he's right. It *is* only fair.

> *Beat.*

I volunteer to take the first shift. I want to drive now before I get tired. But as we pull out of Calgary and head south, I realize it's also because somewhere deep inside maybe I want to be at the

31

wheel when we pass High River. I give the old hometown a little silent nod, a little silent salute in my head as we drive by it, invisible in the inky darkness. It helped launch this whole thing, after all. I don't dare tell Kevin and Hilary about my camping trip down to the Lions Club though.

Besides, we have something much more important to talk about.

The border.

Honestly, this has been weighing on my mind for weeks. Online in Burning Man chat groups, people say to lie. But as I point out, don't you think it will seem strange that a sixty-three-year-old woman is going camping with her son and his friend who is a girl but is not his girlfriend? With hula hoops, fourteen flats of water . . . and a furry bike.

And an eight-foot-long fish kite, Hilary helpfully mentions.

Shit. We look like art terrorists.

Group Decision Number Two: We have to be honest at the border.

Huge mistake. As soon as we mention Burning Man, we're hauled out of line and two grim-faced border guards tell us to go inside and wait while they check our vehicle.

Sit there. Passports please?

As I hand mine over, I can see my hands are shaking. Violently. Oh God, I look guilty. The room's lit by horrible, bright fluorescent lights, just like in a movie. That's when I notice the huge sign on the wall that says we're being continually monitored. I start to think of all the things they might find in the Jag and wonder if any of it is prohibited in the States. Pastels? Handi Wipes? Apples? Can you bring Canadian fruit over the border? I inch over to the garbage and quietly throw three possibly illegal McIntosh apples out of my purse.

I'm interrupted by the guards coming back in and demanding if we'd ever done drugs or been convicted of anything. Hilary is indignant. *No*, she says firmly. *Absolutely not.* They turn to me.

Well . . . the thing is, I did smoke some pot in the sixties, but I was in art school, so that was bound to happen, and that was a long time ago, and it wasn't much, and I haven't done it since, and in fact it never agreed with me, I much prefer red wine . . . But before I can finish Kevin says, *I was caught with some pot once but not charged or convicted.*

One of the guards sees my face: *News to you, Mom?*

The other guard crosses to a computer, checks, nods and says:

Yep. That's true. It was only a few grams, so you weren't charged. Thanks for being honest.

And before I can pick my jaw up off the floor, they hand us our passports back and we're through. Holy shit.

It's 3 a.m.

And we're in the most inhospitable town in America. Sunburst, Montana.

Okay, I don't know how to describe it, but even though it's pitch black, I can tell nobody waters their lawns. There are empty trucks everywhere but not a single person on the streets. Not a single light. Not a soul in town.

There are no campgrounds, so Kevin says we'll just have to pull over and sleep on the side of the road. I've never done that. It seems so *illegal*, but it is the middle of the night, and we're exhausted. He's right. We have no choice. Even so, Kevin's edgy too. Right before we go to sleep, he leans over and whispers: *This is the town in the movie where everyone gets killed.*

I barely sleep. Soon as the sun is up. I make us all a quick pile of toast and fried eggs, but Hilary says:

Oh, no thanks. I'm on a cleansing diet.

That doesn't really make a lot of sense to me, given where we're going, but she's packed some organic juice, so she has that, and we hit the road to Great Falls.

Looking out the window, in the bright sunlight, I'm amazed. Montana is beautiful. Canyons.

Big blue open sky. Winding rivers. And in the distance, these incredible mountains. And you start to feel it. The desert is coming.

We stop for lunch in a tacky diner in Great Falls. Hilary asks for miso soup and microgreens, but they can't seem to help her out, so she has apple juice and a Caesar salad instead.

I don't know why, but sitting there in our booth, I start to picture us like we're a group of outlaws on the run. Somehow, picturing us as characters helps my nerves. Okay, I say, leaning in on my arm like I'm in a really cool road movie: What's next?

Tires, it turns out. Group Decision Number Three: We need tires. Kevin says he saw what looked like a mechanic's shop down the street. Hilary says that's perfect, she spied a costume store a few doors down. *We can kill two birds with one stone: costumes and tires.*

I imagine it's going to be just like Don's Hobby Shop, back in Calgary. An amazing mishmash of feathers and beads, Halloween costumes and makeup.

As we open the door, Kevin speaks first. *Holy shit this is a sex shop and I'm here with my mother.*

Hilary says, *Oh, c'mon, we need to get some costumes. Who cares?*

I don't say anything.

I have never been in a store like this before. A *Love Shop*. I'm not a prude, but I don't go searching out sex stores in Calgary. But it's not creepy inside at all. In fact, there are two fresh-faced young girls working the till.

Can we help you?

Well, actually, we need some tires.

Wow! That's a different kind of rubber than we're used to selling.

But they offer to help. So while Kevin talks to them about tires and Hilary checks out the wig section, I just . . . wander around . . .

Rubber body suits.

We're going to a desert. No. Too sweaty.

Bondage leather and spikes.

No. Too . . . bondage-y.

School-girl outfits.

Oh dear.

Do you need some help?

It's one of the girls from the front, standing next to me.

Um. Okay. What's your most popular costume?

Oh. That's a good question. Hey, Janelle, the lady wants to know . . . what's our most popular costume?

I dunno, Janelle shouts back, *maybe like sexy Batgirl? Ooh, or no . . . Wonder Woman?*

Oh. My. God. That's Kevin. He just realized the lady who wants to know is not Hilary, but his mother.

No . . . Janelle changes her mind one more time, *it's gotta be the French maid.*

Mom!

I end up buying a white-and-gold mask. Kind of like the one the Lone Ranger wore. A hula skirt. And a feather boa. Kevin says he will be traumatized every time I wear them, but I don't care. I like my purchases. They're multi-purpose. They're versatile. They're like a good scarf. They go with everything.

Somehow, those girls work some magic. They not only find us tires, but two nice young guys to put them on. They're good, because in no time they have us back on the Montana road again. Kevin at the wheel for his turn.

Highway 15. Up into the mountains. Through Helena. Butte. Dillon. And then into Idaho. Idaho Falls. Across a big river into Blackfoot. And finally into Pocatello. There, we head west through American Falls to Twin Falls, crossing the border into Nevada through a tiny town called Jackpot.

I'm actually kind of amazed at myself. I've never stayed awake this long in a car in my entire life. It must be the adrenaline. Or the five coffees I drank at that diner. Or the knot of fear hiding in the pit of my stomach. Thankfully, Hilary's up next to drive. As we do the switchover, we make Group Decision Number Four. It's unexpected, but Kevin has looked at his watch.

Shit!

What, Kev? What's going on?

We lost way more time on the tires than I thought. We gotta go as far as we can today. If we don't, we won't be there for opening.

After everything we've been through? No way that's going to happen. So we drive. And drive. And drive. But by 4 a.m., none of us can stay awake. And once again we're hitting a tiny town in the middle of the night with no plans of where we're going to stay. I can feel my blood pressure rising. I cannot do another night in a place like Sunburst.

And we're almost out of gas. It's Hilary. I can hear the panic starting in her voice now too.

Suddenly, I remember something. That thing my American cousins, the Johnsons, gave me years ago when we went to visit them in Montana . . . in case of emergency. I wrench open the glove compartment and start to dig.

Mom, what's going on?

And yes! There it is. My dog-eared Walmart Atlas, a guide and road map of the United States of America.

When he gave it to Eugene and me, Bob said very solemnly: *This is something you should hold onto your whole life. As fellow "road people," I can guarantee it will come in handy one day when you least expect it.* And here it was. The moment.

I tear it open and start searching for Nevada. And *find* it. Yes! I start throwing out instructions: Hilary, turn right on the I-80. And shockingly . . . she does.

And there, up ahead, I see the familiar blue glow. I have never been so happy to see a Walmart Supercentre in my entire life.

Brightly lit, with a gas station open at 4 a.m., with a water tap available for campers, and situated in the middle of the Nevada desert as it is, here in Winnemucca on Potato Road, Walmart is our oasis.

We leap out and gas up. We throw out my Astroturf carpet and our chairs. Kevin is pacing outside the Jag. He seems deeply disturbed.

Kev, what's wrong?

Mom. I thought you knew how I feel about Walmart.

What are you talking about?

What am I talking about? I fundamentally oppose everything Walmart stands for. I . . . I . . .

I can see it in his eyes. I know this look. Kevin. I totally understand. It's just sometimes desperate times call for desperate measures. I promise. No one will ever find out.

I sit him down in his camping chair. Then I do the only thing that I know works, honed from years of experience of road trips with my kids. I go inside and come back with an armload of hoagies from the twenty-four-hour deli. Even he can't resist the smell of hot meat. Hilary too, who seems to be letting go of her cleansing diet. All she says as I hand her a sandwich is: *I need this in my life.* And then we sleep. A luxurious four whole hours. Relaxed. Safe. Thanks be to Walmart.

By 8:30 a.m., I announce I want to drive into Reno.

Kev and Hilary are surprised, but I'm rejuvenated. I can feel it. The adrenaline starting to flow back into my veins.

As I pull out, we start to see art cars being hauled on trailers behind RVs and old VW camping vans. A car passes us, packed solid to the roof with naked mannequins. Small U-Haul trailers go by loaded with poles and tents. They're all Burners. And we're Burners. All on the road to Reno.

Reno is swarming. This is the last place to stock up and they know it. Every store and gas station has mountains of water piled outside. Dried food and canned goods piled inside.

But Kevin only seems to be stocking up on booze. I find him piling vodka, rye, and flats of beer into a cart. Just for the three of us? What are we going to eat?

Don't worry, Ma. People give food away all the time.

Just in case, I grab a bunch of Ichiban noodle cups to add to our Costco stash. I can't help it. I'm a mom.

Burning Man opens their gates at midnight. And somehow, by the skin of our teeth, we've made it. We join the lineup and start the all-night crawl to Black Rock City.

The cars go on forever. Miles and miles and miles of cars. Here in the middle of the deep desert, there's no light. Pitch black. Just the twinkling of long lines of cars as we inch forward. A multi-strand necklace of teeny tiny sparkling diamonds.

Then, suddenly, we start moving. Like, really moving.

Everyone starts cheering. The first rays of light break, and people begin to abandon their cars and walk beside them, taking in the light as it comes over the mountains. People start dancing. And for the first time since we left Calgary, I cry. I miss Eugene. I miss him so much. He was the one who started it all by saying to me once, years ago, that he wanted to come, and somehow he planted a seed in my head, and this is a moment I thought we'd do together one day. Oh fuck. I wish you were here.

She gathers herself.

One thing about Burning Man . . . is there are a lot of ceremonies involved. I had no idea about this. When we're almost at the entrance, Kevin suddenly seems to feel the need to fill us in.

Okay, okay, just so you know, if it's your first time, when you go through the gate, they're gonna ring this bell and then you roll in the dust. It's like a . . . ritual.

But, Kevin, I don't want to do that. I'm prepared to get dirty over ten days, but I'd like to start off clean.

I don't know what to say, Ma.

No thank you. That's what I'm going to say if they ask me. Thanks but no thanks!

But before I can gather any more thoughts, we're at a wall of flag-marked gates. And we're waved into a greeting station. Our greeter is a tall man with long white hair and a beard wearing a voluminous rainbow muumuu. Sure enough, he asks if any of us are first-timers. I look at Kevin and Hilary. They don't say anything. I think they're just taking in his look. So . . . I raise my hand.

I am . . .

Radical Gandalf steps forward, takes me by both hands, and looks into my eyes. Intensely. Like he's looking into my soul. Then he asks me gently: *Would you like to ring a Buddhist prayer bell and roll in the dust as a way of introducing yourself and your bodily vessel to the sacred desert?*

I don't know why. There's just something about the way he says it, and how angelic he looks, and how kindly he speaks, and how epic this all seems, and I don't know . . . I just can't help myself.

Yes! Yes I would!

Mom? What happened to your pledge to stay clean?

Oh, Kev, I don't know. It's just, we made it. And I hug him. And you're so nice, I say to the old guy. And I hug him too. And . . . and . . . it's Burning Man. And I hug Hilary.

She's also feeling the spirit, so the two of us ring the damn bell and roll in the dust like a couple of happy puppies.

Turns out Kevin didn't have to. Because he'd been before. Our greeter gives him the same intense look, but coupled with a warm bear hug. *Welcome back, Kevin. Welcome home.*

And that's it. We passed the test. We made the transition. We have been granted entrance.

Burning Man.

ACT II

Now, I don't know if you've ever seen a picture of Burning Man from above, like from a helicopter, or one of those drones—it looks so organized. It's all arranged like three quarters of a circle, or a rising sun. All facing this huge wooden statue of "the Man." From above, you can see where all the streets are so nicely laid out. And all the thought and care and work that has gone into organizing it. It makes a kind of beautiful sense.

On the ground, it's a different story.

Within those beautifully laid out streets and arcs, everyone is just crammed in. At any angle. Parked like drunken uncles on someone's front lawn. And you can't see how well-planned anything is. Everything you're seeing is through a cloud of gritty, choking dust and sand.

Somehow, through the chaos, Kevin gets a text. His friends with the rig are already in. They try to describe where they are, but it's impossible. So we just drive up and down the arcing streets until suddenly Hilary yells. *Holy shit! There they are!*

And there is the huge truck, the semi, in a prime spot.

I roll to a slow stop.

This is it. Kevin and Hilary jump out, ready to spot me. But I wave them away. Because this is how it's got to be. Just me and the Jag.

Well, girl, here we are.

I step on the brake and put it into reverse when suddenly I catch a glimpse of myself in the rear-view mirror. I almost don't recognize that woman as me. My hair is a mess, I don't have any makeup, but also I . . . I don't look scared. This past year I've gotten so used to seeing a frightened look on my face, I forgot what I really look like. And what I look like right now is . . . determined. Because, well . . . I am. Because you can do this, Dorth. And I think back to that guy at Northland Mall, and that old couple at the campground, and all those long nights at CrossIron Mills and Parveen making his reverse gesture, and I take a deep breath and look myself straight in the eyes. Dorothy, just frickin' park this sucker.

As I do, I realize that there are no parking spots at Burning Man. In fact, there are no lines whatsoever. There are also no trees . . . or cement barriers . . . or hills . . . all my worst fears . . . and in fact everyone is parked horribly, so . . . shit . . . it's way easier than I ever thought possible. I just back it up so that we're one side of a rough circle with the semi and another friend's tent. And just like that, I have parked the Jag at Burning Man!

Woohoo!!

* * * * *

Later that night, as the adrenaline has worn off, I look around and realize I seem to have a good thirty to forty years on everyone. That's when this little negative thought sneaks in.

I made Kevin bring his mom to Burning Man.

I made my son bring his mom to Burning Man.

And suddenly, I don't know . . . I start to feel really bad.

I need Kevin—God knows I need him—but I don't want to be a burden. And poor kid, he's had a hell of a year too. He needs to have his own kind of personal experience as much as I do.

So in a quiet moment, I pull him aside and I say: Look . . . you don't have to babysit me, you know. You show me how to get around, and then we don't always have to be together. I can go off on my own. As long as I can find my way back, I'll be fine.

Ma. This is where the problem lies. You finding your way back. Remember Japan?

> *She looks at the audience.*

My kids are always bringing up that damn trip to Japan.

> *She looks back to the audience. Finally, she relents.*

Okay, fine. It was only my second trip overseas. I don't know what happened, but when Kevin took us up to the remote rural village where he lived, teaching English for the JET Programme, everything I'd learned at my Japanese For Busy People class just flew out of my head. It's not my fault. Japanese is hard. Especially if you didn't grow up hearing it, like Eugene did. The two of us had signed up with such good intentions, but then . . . I don't know . . . we just got too busy.

So, that's how I ended up in a tiny apartment, in the middle of a rice paddy, in the mountains of Japan, bawling my eyes out. Because I could not for the life of me remember the name of the town where Kevin was living. He was like an interrogator.

Ma, what's going to happen if you get lost and they ask you where you're staying?

I have no idea.

You need to tell them where you live. So, right now, say it, where are we?

Kevin, no. I . . . Um . . . Ko . . . tomi.

No! I do not live in Ko-tomi.

Shit. Okay. Ki . . . nomi.

No.

Katakana?

That is not a place! That is a way of writing down Japanese.

At this point, I think Kevin was face down on the table. He was having more trouble teaching me than his four-year-old students.

I was in full panic mode by now. Jason had had to stay in Calgary. Eugene wasn't due to join us for another week. Kevin had to teach. Mieko had people to meet. I couldn't just sit in an apartment in the middle of a rice paddy for seven days.

And that's when it came to him. *Wait, wait, wait . . . try it this way . . . if you want to go home-ie? Try . . . ??*

. . . Koumi?

Holy shit, Kev, you're a genius.

That's Mieko. I think at that point she was also face down on the table. This became their solution to teaching me Japanese. The two of them come up with all kinds of rhymes.

Hot diggity. *Onigiri.* For when I wanted to order rice balls.

If you want to get your food on, order *udon.*

So I guess what I'm saying is . . . here at Burning Man, in the midst of all this chaos, Kevin's fear of me getting lost is . . . valid.

So, that first night at Burning Man, we make a plan.

We start by looking around us. What could we use as a signpost to find the camp? My fish mobile *is* on the large side and would be visible once you were within about twenty feet of the Jag, but Kevin was right, it's not big enough to be a landmark in this sea of humanity. Damn.

And suddenly there it was. A giant four-storey tower a group had somehow impossibly erected, with a neon arrow pointing down. At an enormous penis sculpture.

It was perfect. Kev, I won't get lost because . . . if I want to get cleaner, I'll just search for the . . . weiner.

Kevin laughed so hard I thought he was going to choke.

*So . . . if you want to find your bunk? You'll head right for the
. . . junk?*

Even Hilary got into it. *If you don't want to go wrong, go look for
the . . . shlong.*

Kev. It worked in Japan. It'll work here. And if you're really ner-
vous, just write down where we are on a piece of paper. I promise,
I'll tie it around my neck and if I get lost I'll ask for directions.
Kevin, I've come all this way because I want to . . . no, I actually
need . . . to do things on my own.

He looks at me. I can tell he still thinks this is a very bad idea. But
I can also tell he kind of understands. He writes down our coordi-
nates on a piece of paper and hands it over.

> *Beat. She silently mouths the words to him.*

Thank you.

Day One.

Picture this. It's noon. I'm standing on the playa. To my left, Kevin and
Hilary. To my right, two of his friends from the electronic music scene.

One of them has the festival directory in his hand, reading out
potential events for us to walk to and experience. We all listen with
rapt attention.

Fisting 101.

What's that?

Kevin shoots his grinning friend the stink eye. *Mom. It's okay. We are not going there.*

Grilled Cheese Sandwiches.

I vote to go to Grilled Cheese Sandwiches! Hilary has really gotten into food since giving up her cleansing diet.

I lean in and scan the page. Hmn. Geocaching, Sword Training, or Art Pirates all sound interesting to me.

Kevin makes a face. *I'd rather check out HipHopHappyHour or Hellevator.*

Well, I throw out . . . maybe it's time we all go our separate ways.

And it happens. We agree to split up.

* * * * *

She looks around. She's frozen.

The thing is, if I'm honest with you, I've never been a risk-taker. Ever. Eugene was the one with big ideas. He was the one who convinced me to move to Toronto and live in Kensington Market without any running hot water. Who started his own design business in *Calgary*. Who thought it was a good idea to buy a house on Christmas Eve. My whole life, I marvelled at his ability to jump off a cliff with complete confidence. *How hard can it be?* was what he always said.

When a person like that is at your side, the world doesn't feel so scary. You get used to their bravery and you jump with them.

But now . . .

Now.

Here I am.

My first adventure. Alone.

Where do *I* want to go?

* * * * *

Beat.

I just start walking.

I don't have a plan, so I just walk down our street, and then turn down another avenue, and take another turn, and another, until I work my way to the outside of the festival and I'm faced with the open desert. It's funny: when you're in the middle of chaos, you don't realize the vast, bare space around you.

It's empty.

Except . . . in the far, far distance, I catch sight of something. A structure coming in and out of focus through the blowing sand

and the heat waves like a mirage. The tiny black dots moving around at the base must be people. It's the Temple. The Temple is one of the things they set up every year, but each year it has a different theme and design.

So I just start walking towards it.

I'm walking for ages when I come upon a tiny sand-coloured tent. It blends in so perfectly I don't see it until I'm almost on top of it. It's literally in the middle of nowhere, halfway between the festival and the Temple.

I realize it's just one of those simple plastic tents you see at a street festival. You know, like a food booth. But with four walls. Painted to match the sand. There's no sign outside, no indication of what it is, except . . . a small rectangular welcome mat.

She enters.

It's a bar. Dark velvet-draped walls. Old Master style paintings hung on three sides. A beautiful antique wooden counter, with a wall of bottles arranged behind it. As if on cue, a man appears, popping up from below the counter, polishing a glass. He's dressed like an old-time bartender with garters on his sleeves. He smiles: *What can I get you?*

I usually just ask for something fruity, like a cider, but this is a proper bar.

She thinks.

A Shirley Temple please.

What a perfect choice. He gets a tall glass, fills it with chunks of frosty ice, and starts building. First a layer of orange juice then lemon-lime soda. Then a thick layer of grenadine that slowly sinks to the bottom. He tops it off with a single perfect maraschino cherry.

What is this place?

> *He shrugs modestly.*

My small gift. The chaos of the playa is astonishing, but I believe creating a quiet spot for a person to have a drink and gather themselves, is . . . essential.

What do you *think?*

> *She drinks.*

It is.

* * * * *

It's funny. The Temple is not at all what I expected. It's not some crazy *Mad Max* Thunderdome like I imagined. It's . . . incredibly beautiful. It almost looks like a Middle Eastern mosque, with a huge white and gold central minaret tower with tall arched windows. It's amazing to me that humans can build this in the middle of an empty desert.

It's peaceful inside. Quiet and hushed, just like any grand cathedral in Europe. The ceiling is spectacular. Fashioned out of hundreds of panels of carved wood. Delicate as handmade Italian lace. The floor is bare, just regular playa sand, but actually you can't see that at all because it's covered by hundreds of people just lying on their backs looking up. Some seem to be meditating or sleeping. Others just lying with their eyes open . . . thinking.

I walk carefully around the edge and read things people have written on the walls. It's only the first day but it's already filling up with all kinds of personal things: statements, pictures. Some are happy, like baby and wedding pictures . . . things people want to remember and celebrate, but others are sadder. There is a whole tribute written to a one-eyed cat who had a short but impactful life. A farewell to a cancerous tumour. And brief, enigmatic phrases like "I'm sorry," "No More Fear," and "Now, I am free." And of course there are lots of names, dates, and hearts. People's loved ones. Loved ones being mourned and missed.

I'm suddenly overwhelmed, so I find a corner to myself.

She lies on the floor and looks up.

It's funny that we build these spaces for ourselves. That we search for these spaces. Over and over. In a continuous line back to the beginning of time. Even in the earliest days humans must have sat in caves and thought some of these same things in places where they drew pictures. Built fires. Ate food. And lay on the floor and looked up, lost in their thoughts just like all these people are doing . . . like I'm doing.

Lying there, my mind clears for a moment. I can just hear the sound of some soft chimes in the distance, and something lets go, and that's enough to take the world away. And for a moment, I don't feel sad. I don't feel empty. I feel like I'm one with everyone else in the room. We breathe together.

And that's when it comes to me.

* * * *

By the time I make my way back to camp, thanks to the help of a few strangers, our rhymes, and the giant neon arrow, Kevin is waiting for me. He claims he was looking for his friend, but I think he was worried. He makes me some instant noodles while I tell him about the Temple.

Sounds awesome. So . . . what did you bring back?

What do you mean?

MOOP, *Ma.*

MOOP?

Yeah, MOOP. M-O-O-P.

Turns out MOOP is something very particular to Burning Man. It stands for Matter Out Of Place. And Leaving No Trace is one of the central rules of Burning Man. One of the main goals of the whole event is to leave the desert exactly as it was before we were here.

So MOOP is basically anything you find on the ground. It could be a sequin, a feather, a piece of trash. Anything out of place in the desert. Kevin says people make it kind of a game. They collect MOOP all day and then compare what they found with their camp mates when they get home.

I reach into my pocket and pull out a puka shell and a Vegas casino chip. I don't even remember where I picked them up.

Pure you, Mom. Brought MOOP back before you even knew what it was. Always an early adopter.

Actually, I've always been this way. Since I was a kid. My house is packed with little things. Things I find on dog walks, on beach walks, on any walk, really. It's weird the things you discover about yourself. Even at this age . . . I'm a MOOP collector.

Eugene was even worse. He loved to include found objects in his art. Mixed Media, they call it. We'd be driving somewhere and he'd slam on the brakes and jump out and retrieve an old work glove off the road. And in it would go. One of his pieces featured a whole grid of chipped antique porcelain doll heads he'd found at a junk store. Mieko called it *Dead Baby Heads* when she was little. It gave all the kids nightmares, but it was strangely beautiful.

When Mieko was in grade twelve, Eugene took her to see Laurie Anderson's movie *Home of the Brave* at the Plaza, and on the way home he made her stop and stand watch while he ripped a bulletin board off the wall of the ancient old laundromat on 10th Street.

Dad! What are you doing?

The people who own this laundromat don't appreciate this. Look at it. He pointed at the swear words and hearts and phone numbers that covered the old thing. *This has life. It has character. They won't even notice.*

Apparently, a couple of students inside the laundromat did notice, however, and headed for the emergency phone on the wall. That's when Eugene gave her a big grin and ran for the van. Mieko told me what happened as soon as they got home. She wanted me to agree with her. And he *was* wrong . . . of course. He shouldn't have taken it. But . . . he was also right.

He saw the beauty in it.

He made it art.

Late that night, I get my Inspire journal and watercolours out. And I just start painting. I paint pages and pages and pages. Big swooping colourful swirls. Impressions of the desert. And then I write on top of them:

EVERYONE AND EVERYTHING HAS SOMETHING TO OFFER.

YOU ARE NOT JUST MOOP.

* * * * *

Day Two.

The day started off innocently enough. My only goal for the day was to get to Camp Big Pants.

It was the camp of some people that my daughter knew.

You should look them up, Mom. They're pretty cool. Theatre designers.

My confidence was up, so I thought, all right, Dazzle, let's see if we can find them. Shockingly, Kevin and Hilary want to come. Can you believe it? *They* want to tag along with *me*.

She pulls out Dazzle.

Okay, girl, you ready?

She cycles.

This is . . . almost fun.

We hadn't gotten far when a naked man passes me on a bike. Then another. And I'm thinking . . . wow, these guys really travel in packs. Then three more go by. Then nine. Then it's a tsunami, and I am suddenly engulfed in a wave of arms and legs and penises and hula skirts. Okay, only one hula skirt. Mine.

That damn hula skirt was my undoing. I should have taken into consideration that I was going to ride my bike and gone for a tutu instead. I think while I was trying to keep my eye on Kevin and Hilary, who were just in front of me, the rattan strands of the skirt must have worked their way into my gears, which twisted them into my cogs, which clotheslined me, and pretty soon I was flying ass over teakettle through a sea of naked men.

I land with a brutal thump. Concerned nude men immediately surround me.

Are you okay? You really took a tumble. Anything broken?

I was so winded, and I also didn't know where to look, so I just lay in the sand, frozen, staring straight up. If I could have spoken, I think I would have said: Wow, you're all so nice. And considerate. You would think that it would be strange to be helped by a gang of naked male cyclists, but it's actually kind of sweet and wholesome.

At least that's what I was thinking.

I wasn't saying any of this out loud because I was gasping for air, so I think they thought I had some sort of brain injury. Thankfully, a small truck drives by. The guys frantically wave it over and a volunteer jumps out. Part of the Emergency Services crew. She kneels next to me.

Hi there. My name is Lisa. How are you feeling? Are you okay?

> *She smiles and nods.*

Oh good. Maybe you're just in a little shock. The guys say you took a real tumble. You did manage to wipe out in the middle of the annual Naked Man Bike Parade. That's enough to make anyone speechless for a bit, hey?

> *She tries to speak.*

. . . hula skirt . . .

Yeah. Takes people down on bikes every year. Can you sit up?

I do, and one of the guys yells to the group. *The lady's up!* And they all cheer. And Lisa helps me off to the side as the bike parade restarts. There are hundreds of them. Two of the guys retrieve Dazzle and clear the strands of my skirt out of my chain and set her up on her bike stand. They wave cheerfully. *So glad you're okay! Hope you have a good festival!* They seem so normal I almost forget they're buck naked. And then they're gone. Swallowed up in a cloud of dust.

Once Lisa confirms that I seem to be okay, she tells me to come in to Centre Camp if I feel dizzy or sick later. I promise her that I will head straight back to my camp and take it easy for the rest of the day.

Later I discover I'm covered in bruises.

Hula skirts. Bikes. Not friends. Lesson learned.

Kevin feels terrible that he missed my big crash. He and Hilary had just kept on cycling. It was only when they got really lost and stopped for directions that they realized I wasn't there.

What can I say? I lost you both too. I was in a sea of balls.

But Kevin looks stricken. I hug him. Don't worry. I'm tougher than you think.

Hey. I do have a surprise though, Mom. To make up for it, we're going to bring you into the fold.

He gives me some ear plugs and grins. *Our camp's gift to Burning Man, Ma. The Boom of Doom.*

*Music starts to pound. They are in the middle of the
electronic music area their camp has set up.*

Ma! Isn't this awesome?

It *is* awesome. The beat is so powerful I can feel the hairs on my
arms vibrating. It's sort of hypnotic. Everyone is dancing, so I don't
know . . . I just start to . . .

She starts to dance. She has a lot of moves.

Hilary yells: *Whoa. Where did you learn all these cool moves
Dorothy?*

ZUMBA!!

She and Kevin look at me blankly. They have no idea what I'm
talking about. Where do you live? I shout. Under a mushroom?
Zumba? It's HUGE. It's a worldwide phenomenon. It's an exercise
class, but it's also dance. It's at the Y. It's amazing. You two should
come sometime. It's every Thursday. Our teacher, Rain? She's
amazing. She really gets us all going. Kids, teenagers. Even the
really old ladies. She gets like eighty of us going at one time. Then
we go for coffee after class.

Hilary's sold. *I'd come. Can I wear wings?*

Sure, Rain would be really into that.

Well, all those Zumba classes paid off, because after what seemed
like just a few songs, Kevin is more out of breath than me. *Shit,*

you're a dancing machine, Mom. You haven't taken a break in hours. Make sure you stay hydrated, keep drinking.

And I do. But that brings my great start to a quick end. It would be one thing if I had been sucking back water like I do at the Y, but here people only seem to give me drinks that are half hard liquor. I start to feel like I'm in one of those depression-era dance offs. I'm covered in sweat and sand, which is turning into paste. My headband is falling off. I've lost an earplug. It feels like we've been here for days.

I gotta go to bed, I say to Kevin.

But, Mom, it's only four.

Yeah, but I'm sixty-three!

Oh shit. Right.

I head for the Jag. I have never been so happy to see my bed and my quilt and my pyjamas. I like this electronic music stuff, but I love sleep more.

★ ★ ★ ★ ★

The next day I decide to really get into the art projects. People get so caught up in the crazy clothes people wear and all the antics, I think they forget sometimes that, at its heart, Burning Man is an art festival.

I hear that someone has made a Trojan Horse. So cool. It was conceived at the Banff Centre, not far from my house in Calgary. Small world.

So that is my goal for the day. Find the horse!

When I finally see it, wow! It's about five storeys high. At the base, a small group is gathered. A beautiful art car pulls up and a lady tells everyone to get on board. She announces they are going to do a drive around the horse while giving a talk about it. So I jump right on. There is a very glamorous gold throne on top of the car, so I climb up and sit.

That's when the lady says, *I'm so sorry, I'm the coordinator and I just noticed that you don't have a tag. This car is just for media. This is a press conference.* I don't know what comes over me, but I say: Well, I'm Dorothy, and I'm an artist and I'm very interested in this horse. And I give her one of my artist trading cards. She's a bit taken aback. *Oh. Well, I guess that's fine then.* A young man in a plaid button-up shirt and crisp new black jeans crawls up and sits next to me on the throne. I can tell he really likes to iron. He says, *I don't know why they assigned me to Burning Man. I live in Manhattan.*

Assigned you to come?

New York Times. *Who are you?*

That's what I've been wondering.

I'm . . . just a person, I say. From Calgary.

I'm Dorothy.

* * * * *

After the Trojan Horse talk, I don't know why . . . but I head back to the Temple.

For some reason, today it's full of naked people dancing. It's funny, sometimes Burning Man is kind of like being in the change room at the Y. You never know who is going to show up, and everyone is naked, but it's just not a big deal. I think people just want to feel . . . free.

I find a different corner than on my first visit.

A man, maybe in his forties, has just written something on the wall and now is sitting looking at his hands.

I guess he noticed me looking at him and felt he had to say something. *I'm . . . I'm just working through my sadness about my girlfriend leaving me.*

Oh, I said. I see.

How about you?

    Beat.

I'm grieving.

    Beat.

For my husband.

Beat.

He died last year.

Shit. I'm sorry.

Yeah. Me too.

Neither of us needed to say anything more. We both just nodded.

And he went back to staring at his hands. And I went back to thinking about Eugene, and we sat there together in the Temple.

Some people say it's better if it happens fast. The suffering, if there is any, is shorter. There's no agonizing struggle and wait.

Others say, though, if it happens slowly, that gives you more time to talk, to say goodbye. To wrap your head around the enormity of it. The scale of what it is you are being asked to digest.

The sheer size of what is coming.

But the truth is, I don't think it matters how it happens.

No matter how it happens, you *never* really see it coming. You're never ready.

You're never ever ready.

Especially for the loneliness that follows.

The upending of everything you thought would continue forever.

The tectonic shift.

As you face . . .

Your life. Your new life.

Alone.

* * * * *

Late that night, I was still thinking about the Temple when the Aussies from next door came over and said, *I reckon you might want to try this.*

We had just finished up supper, and everyone seemed to be having some, like it was an after-dinner coffee. So . . . I don't know what came over me, but . . . I smoke a bit.

And it was . . . fine. At first. At first I didn't actually feel anything at all. The pipe went around again. Okay, just one more puff, I said. Everyone kept on chatting and talking.

But then I start to feel something. Something. Strange. I try to sit quietly for a while, hoping it will pass. But it doesn't. It just grows and grows.

Um, I have to go, I say, and I guess I make a pretty urgent beeline for the Jag, because someone must have gone and told Kevin. He pops his head into the RV.

Momma? Are you okay?

Kevin, I have no idea how to answer that question.

He comes over to the bed and looks into my eyes . . .

    He laughs.

Wow, you've really done a number on yourself. Congrats, Ma, you just got junior high stoned. You've smoked too much.

I don't know what to say, so I just start crying. *Aw, don't feel bad. Everyone does it at some point.* He doesn't seem concerned at all. He pats my hand: *Don't worry. You're amongst friends.*

No I'm not. I'm amongst 55,000 strangers. In Nevada.

But the people here at our camp are my friends, and they all really like you, so they're your friends too. Do you want some orange juice? Do you want me to leave you? So you can get some sleep?

Kevin, don't leave. And stop talking. I can't answer questions right now. I can't form answers anymore. Just . . . don't go.

So he sits there on the floor next to me while I lie there, the bed spinning. All I can think about is Eugene. One of the very first dates he took me on. 1967. I was eighteen. He was twenty-two. He took me down to the Bow River to see some old, wrecked, rotting cars he'd found.

Aren't they cool? He said. *Look at the rust on them.* He always found rust particularly beautiful.

And they were beautiful. Old cars from the forties maybe. Big swooping curves. Chrome accents. I know some people would have thought this was a weird thing to take your potential girl-friend to go and see, but I thought it was . . . so romantic . . .

We sit on the banks of the river and smoke a bit of pot, but honestly it gets in the way of what we really want to do. So we toss the joint away and pull out our sketch pads and some watercolours and paint.

We don't need drugs to fall in love.

We just need art.

* * * * *

The burns happen over three days.

First, on the Friday, the warm-up burn. This year, the Trojan Horse.

It starts with a guy shooting a lit arrow, setting it on fire. Then fire-works start bursting out of it.

Then thousands of fire spinners are suddenly all around us. You just don't see this kind of thing in Calgary.

Actually, I don't think you see this kind of thing anywhere but here.

Looking around, I realize, we have become a community.

Made up of people looking for a place they can watch a Trojan Horse burn till dawn.

* * * * *

Saturday night is the release of the Man.

This is the image everyone thinks of when they think of
Burning Man.

First everyone creates a gigantic circle around the sculpture. And
doing that simple act makes you realize how many people are
really here. The circle is enormous.

Then the buildup begins. Gymnastics. Aerials. Basically anything
that can be lit on fire seems to be spun by someone somewhere. A
whole show put on by volunteers.

The event is so big no one can really say much, 'cause no one
would hear, so we all just listen to the music and the noise.

Then suddenly everything quiets down. And everyone who has
been performing, slowly fans out, joining the rest of us, so in that
big circle all the views are the same. No bad seats.

And then . . . they set the Man on fire.

If you've never seen a seventy-five-foot-tall effigy of a man burn
at night in the middle of the desert, I don't know if you fully grasp
what it is to be human. It's spectacular, sure. But more powerful
than that is the way it makes you feel connected to your ancestors.
To everyone who has gone before you. I can imagine what it must
have felt like to bury King Tut in a pyramid. Or what it might feel
like to see the finally completed Great Wall of China snaking out

in front of you. Or what it's like standing on the very top of Machu Picchu.

We all sit together, our whole camp, while it burns. Kevin, Hilary. All the kids. They're all so sweet. Some are wearing my tutus.

As the fire burns down, I notice the young man next to me is crying.

Are you okay? I say.

Yup. He seems embarrassed.

It's okay, I say. It's very emotional.

It's just . . . I didn't think I'd feel this way. I thought this was all kind of corny when I first got here. I work in punk music? You can get kind of cynical working in punk.

Hunh, I say. Well, I don't know about that, but my husband died recently. And that can make you feel pretty cynical about the world too.

I'm sure it can, he says.

And then he tells me that he suffers from depression. I don't know why he's so open with me, but I just try to listen. I think we kind of bond in that moment.

And then he says something that surprises me.

I wish my mom would come to Burning Man.

I feel my heart catch in my throat.

You know what . . . you should be careful what you wish for.

Sometimes moms surprise you.

Sometimes moms surprise themselves.

Sometimes moms do.

She reaches out and holds his hand.

We watch the Man burn all night.

We watch until it's nothing but a pile of smouldering embers.

All the kids are asleep in mounds around me, half on top of each other, like a pile of puppies.

Sitting there, looking at them, I feel like I'm the only person in the world awake.

But I'm not upset.

I feel at peace.

In the morning, that sweet boy invites me to go skating at a roller derby someone had set up on site.

Aw, I say, that is a really nice invitation, but I'm so tired, I think I should have a nap.

I am tired . . . but the truth is, I need time to myself. I need . . . to prepare.

She pulls out a small model of the Temple.

The final day, Sunday, is the Temple burn.

That burn is totally different.

The Friday burn was hedonistic and fun. The Saturday burn of the Man felt epic and primal.

But the Temple feels different.

The Temple is such a quiet meditative place. Like a church. But without pews or clergy. Or a program. Just a beautiful space meant to open up our minds to awe, to memories . . . to the big questions.

By the end of the ten days, the walls are completely full. Every inch covered in words, thoughts, charms, photos, drawings. Every square inch of it.

It's the most visited space at Burning Man.

And I understand why. It symbolizes the most important thing at the festival. The reason we're all really here.

Letting go.

And burning it away into nothing somehow means even more.

It's a recognition of our impermanence. Our impermanence on this earth. Our lives are short. Our flames burn and then they go out.

And I think back to Kevin's original question to me in Calgary.

Ma, why do you want to go to Burning Man?

This is my pilgrimage.

For Eugene.

And I think back to that young man who asked me that question, while we sat on a throne and looked at a Trojan Horse.

Who are you?

And I know this is also my pilgrimage for myself.

It's about feeling all the feelings and then letting them go.

It's about feeling a deep, deep inexplicable love for someone and letting them go.

It's about planning a life and letting it go.

It's about finding your greatest fears and letting them go.

Watching all those things burn away inside the gestural images of a man, a temple, and a horse . . . with a group of people who understand.

Right before the burn I take the plastic bag out of its secret hiding spot in the Jaguar. It's just a regular Superstore bag, but inside it are seven things. Seven paper pads full of my most horrible, sad, terrified thoughts and feelings. Everything that poured out while Eugene lay dying in our bedroom. In our home. As we all held his hands and tried to wrap our heads around what was happening to us.

That night, right before the burn, I put them in the Temple.

I say goodbye to my old life.

She sets the Temple on fire.

Together, along with the audience, she watches it burn.

And I watch it burn.

ACKNOWLEDGEMENTS

I would like to acknowledge the generous support of Workshop West Playwrights' Theatre, fu-GEN Theatre Company, and the Royal Manitoba Theatre Centre in the development of this script. Huge thanks to David Yee, Krista Jackson, Kelly Thornton, and Vern Thiessen for their encouragement and belief along the way. It meant the world.

Huge thanks to all the artists who read the play, dramaturged, offered feedback, or directed readings throughout its development: Brenda Kamino, Diana Belshaw, Jennifer Villaverde, Valerie Planche, Maralyn Ryan, Vanessa Porteous, and most deeply Nicola Lipman.

Love and gratitude to Lisa Horner and Megan McArton, who breathed life into the premiere with such love and caring, and to the entire creative team at the Royal Manitoba Theatre Centre, who put their hearts and souls into the production. Your contributions are part of the fabric of this work.

I would also like to acknowledge the love and support of my kind and patient husband, Kim Clegg, who supported me so deeply through the tragic time of my dad's passing and all that came before and after that. I love you and am lucky to have you as a partner in this grand adventure.

Finally, I would like to acknowledge the incredible generosity and trust of my mother, Dorothy Ouchi, who opened up her heart, her private memories, and even her diaries to me. And to my brothers, Kevin and Jason Ouchi, for encouraging me to share our story and giving me the freedom to portray them in the play. You are brave and loving humans, and I am forever grateful to be your daughter and sister.

Writer, director, dramaturg, and actor, Mieko Ouchi trained at the University of Alberta's BFA Acting Program, the Women in the Director's Chair Program, and the National Screen Institute. Her award-winning films have screened at over thirty festivals, including the Toronto and Vancouver International Film Festivals and Asian American film festivals in San Francisco, New York, Los Angeles, and San Diego. Her plays *The Red Priest (Eight Ways To Say Goodbye)*, *The Blue Light*, *The Dada Play*, *Nisei Blue*, *I Am For You*, *Consent*, *The Silver Arrow*, and *Burning Mom* have been translated into six languages, been finalists for the 4 Play Series at the Old Vic, UK; the Governor General's Literary Award; the Gwen Pharis Ringwood Award; the City of Edmonton Book Prize; and Sterling Awards, and have been recognized with the Carol Bolt Award, Betty Mitchell Awards, and the Enbridge Playwrights Award for Established Canadian Playwright. Her work as a director and dramaturg—both at Concrete Theatre where she was Co-Artistic Director and Artistic Director for thirty-one years, and with writers and companies across the country—spans TYA to indie to large-scale work. Mieko now works as Associate Artistic Director at the Citadel Theatre. She lives in Edmonton with her husband Kim and their dog Nara.

First edition: April 2023
Printed and bound in Canada by Rapido Books, Montreal

"Burning Man" is the registered trademark of Black Rock City LLC, and is
used throughout this book with permission.

Cover art: *Temple of Transition* by Chris Hankins, Diarmaid Horkan, and the
International Arts Megacrew
Temple photo © Scott London, scottlondon.com
Image used with the permission of Burning Man Project
Photo of woman © iStock.com/Koldunov
Jacket design by Kim Clegg
Author photo © Ryan Parker

Playwrights Canada Press
202-269 Richmond St. w.
Toronto, ON
M5V 1X1

416.703.0013
info@playwrightscanada.com
www.playwrightscanada.com